THE ILLUSTRATED Robert Frost

25 ESSENTIAL POEMS

EDITED BY
RYAN G.
VAN CLEAVE

BUSHEL
& PECK
BOOKS

BUSHEL
& PECK
BOOKS

Bushel & Peck Books is dedicated to fighting illiteracy all over the world.
For every book we sell, we donate one to a child in need—book for book.
To nominate a school or organization to receive free books,
please visit www.bushelandpeckbooks.com.

Design and illustration by David Miles.
Type set in Baskerville and Calder.
Collage illustrations were created digitally from various public domain works
and/or elements licensed from Shutterstock.com.

LCCN: TK
ISBN: 9781638191063

First Edition

Printed in China

10 9 8 7 6 5 4 3

Selections

EXPLORING NATURE

Gathering Leaves 6

A Late Walk 8

Leaves Compared with Flowers 11

My November Guest 12

The Onset 14

Mowing 16

Tree at My Window 19

A Prayer in Spring 20

The Oven Bird 23

INNOCENCE & INSPIRATION

The Door in the Dark 27

Hyla Brook 28

Acquainted with the Night 31

Desert Places 33

Birches 34

Nothing Gold Can Stay 37

Flower-Gathering 39

The Need of Being Versed in Country Things 40

CHOICE & CHANGE

Stopping by Woods on a Snowy Evening 44

Fire and Ice 46

The Road Not Taken 49

An Old Man's Winter Night 51

Mending Wall 52

Dust of Snow 54

The Freedom of the Moon 57

The Wood-Pile 58

INTRODUCTION

Welcome to the Illustrated Poets Collection! Here are three suggestions to help you make the most of this book.

SUGGESTION 1: Enjoy the poems. This seems far more important than trying to puzzle out what the author meant (or what other people believe the author meant).

SUGGESTION 2: Engage with the poems by asking questions. Here are three that should prove useful for any poem you encounter:

- *What do you notice about this poem?*

- *How does this poem make you feel?*

- *What else have you read/seen/experienced that connects with this poem?*

You'll also find individual questions suggested for each poem in this book.

SUGGESTION 3: Be your own boss. Read the poems in order or jump around as you see fit. Share them or savor them all by yourself. Say them aloud or whisper their words in your heart.

Poetry makes life better. There is NO wrong way to experience a poem.

So, read on, dear friend. And thank you for choosing poetry.

Ryan G. Van Cleave
Series Editor

PART I

Exploring Nature

GATHERING
LEAVES

Spades take up leaves
No better than spoons,
And bags full of leaves
Are light as balloons.

I make a great noise
Of rustling all day
Like rabbit and deer
Running away.

But the mountains I raise
Elude my embrace,
Flowing over my arms
And into my face.

I may load and unload
Again and again
Till I fill the whole shed,
And what have I then?

Next to nothing for weight,
And since they grew duller
From contact with earth,
Next to nothing for color.

Next to nothing for use,
But a crop is a crop,
And who's to say where
The harvest shall stop?

IMAGINE

If this poem inspired a movie, what type of movie would it be? Comedy? Drama? Action? Something else?

DEFINE

Elude: *avoid*

A LATE WALK

When I go up through the mowing field,
    The headless aftermath,
Smooth-laid like **thatch** with the heavy dew,
    Half closes the garden path.

And when I come to the garden ground,
    The whir of **sober** birds
Up from the tangle of withered weeds
    Is sadder than any words.

A tree beside the wall stands bare,
    But a leaf that lingered brown,
Disturbed, I doubt not, by my thought,
    Comes softly rattling down.

I end not far from my going forth
    By picking the faded blue
Of the last remaining **aster** flower
    To carry again to you.

ENGAGE

*What would make
a late walk "sadder
than any words"?*

*Which phrase—
"garden ground"
or "withered
weeds"—appeals to
you more?*

*Why doesn't the
"you" in the final
line appear earlier
in the poem?*

IMAGINE

*What's another
title you could give
this poem?*

DEFINE

thatch: *straw
roof cover*

sober: *serious*

aster: *purple or
pink daisy*

trees have bloom so small
t as well have none at all.
fe I have come on fern.
are due to have their
ell me which in brief,
er, flower or leaf,
ve the wit to say,
nd flo

LEAVES COMPARED WITH FLOWERS

A tree's leaves may be ever so good,
So may its bark, so may its wood;
But unless you put the right thing to its root
It never will show much flower or fruit.

But I may be one who does not care
Ever to have tree bloom or bear.
Leaves for smooth and bark for rough,
Leaves and bark may be tree enough.

Some giant trees have bloom so small
They might as well have none at all.
Late in life I have come on **fern**.
Now **lichens** are due to have their turn.

I **bade** men tell me which in brief,
Which is fairer, flower or leaf.
They did not have the **wit** to say,
Leaves by night and flowers by day.

Leaves and bark, leaves and bark,
To lean against and hear in the dark.
Petals I may have once pursued.
Leaves are all my darker mood.

MY NOVEMBER GUEST

My Sorrow, when she's here with me,
 Thinks these dark days of autumn rain
Are beautiful as days can be;
She loves the bare, the withered tree;
 She walks the **sodden** pasture lane.

Her pleasure will not let me stay.
 She talks and I am **fain** to **list**:
She's glad the birds are gone away,
She's glad her simple **worsted** gray
 Is silver now with clinging mist.

The desolate, deserted trees,
 The faded earth, the heavy sky,
The beauties she so truly sees,
She thinks I have no eye for these,
 And **vexes** me for reason why.

Not yesterday I learned to know
 The love of bare November days
Before the coming of the snow,
But it were **vain** to tell her so,
 And they are better for her praise.

ENGAGE

Why is "My Sorrow" personified as a woman?

Is the guest only present in November?

Why are "bare November days" "better for her praise"?

IMAGINE

What's your haiku version of this poem? (A haiku only has three lines—the first is five syllables long, the middle has seven, and the last has five.)

DEFINE

sodden: *soaked through*

fain: *eager*

list: *listen*

worsted: *woolen yarn*

vexes: *annoys*

vain: *useless*

THE ONSET

Always the same, when on a fated night
At last the gathered snow lets down as white
As may be in dark woods, and with a song
It shall not make again all winter long
Of hissing on the yet uncovered ground,
I almost stumble looking up and round,
As one who overtaken by the end
Gives up his errand, and lets death descend
Upon him where he is, with nothing done
To evil, no important triumph won,
More than if life had never been begun.

Yet all the **precedent** is on my side:
I know that winter death has never tried
The earth but it has failed: the snow may heap
In long storms an undrifted four feet deep
As measured again maple, birch, and oak,
It cannot check the **peeper**'s silver croak;
And I shall see the snow all go down hill
In water of a slender April **rill**
That flashes tail through last year's withered **brake**
And dead weeds, like a disappearing snake.
Nothing will be left white but here a birch,
And there a clump of houses with a church.

⚙ ENGAGE

How does the title—see the definition of "onset" below—relate to the poem?

At what point does the poem move from sadness and fear to something more hopeful?

What's the importance of the last word ("church") in this poem?

💡 IMAGINE

Poems talk to each other in interesting ways. What does this one say to/about "Stopping By Woods on a Snowy Evening?" (on page 44)?

🔤 DEFINE

Onset: *the start of something, often unpleasant*

precedent: *earlier event that serves as a guide*

peeper: *small tree frog*

rill: *small stream*

brake: *overgrown area*

15

MOWING

There was never a sound beside the wood but one,
And that was my long **scythe** whispering to the ground.
What was it it whispered? I knew not well myself;
Perhaps it was something about the heat of the sun,
Something, perhaps, about the lack of sound—
And that was why it whispered and did not speak.
It was no dream of the gift of idle hours,

Or easy gold at the hand of **fay** or elf:
Anything more than the truth would have seemed too weak
To the earnest love that laid the **swale** in rows,
Not without feeble-pointed spikes of flowers
(Pale **orchises**), and scared a bright green snake.
The fact is the sweetest dream that labor knows.
My long scythe whispered and left the hay to make.

ENGAGE

What do you notice about sounds and silence in this poem?

Since sonnets are usually love poems, and this poem is a sonnet, how might this poem be about love?

What conclusion does the poem offer about the scythe and mowing grass?

IMAGINE

What would your pen say if it could speak?

What about your computer keyboard?

Your shoes?

DEFINE

scythe: *long curved blade that cuts grass*

fay: *fairy*

swale: *low, wet field*

orchises: *purple or pink orchids*

TREE AT MY WINDOW

Tree at my window, window tree,
My sash is lowered when night comes on;
But let there never be curtain drawn
Between you and me.

Vague dream-head lifted out of the ground,
And thing next most **diffuse** to cloud,
Not all your light tongues talking aloud
Could be **profound**.

But, tree, I have seen you taken and tossed,
And if you have seen me when I slept,
You have seen me when I was taken and swept
And all but lost.

That day she put our heads together,
Fate had her imagination about her,
Your head so much concerned with outer,
Mine with inner, weather.

 ENGAGE

Why does this speaker choose to personify the tree?

How would you describe the mood of this poem? Serious, playful, thoughtful, or something else?

What type of weather is "inner" weather?

 IMAGINE

Try to communicate the meaning of a poem through dance. Stomp your feet, move like the wind, or get all twisty. Be creative!

 DEFINE

diffuse: *spread over a large area*

profound: *great understanding*

A PRAYER IN SPRING

Oh, give us pleasure in the flowers today;
And give us not to think so far away
As the uncertain harvest; keep us here
All simply in the springing of the year.

Oh, give us pleasure in the orchard white,
Like nothing else by day, like ghosts by night;
And make us happy in the happy bees,
The swarm **dilating** round the perfect trees.

And make us happy in the darting bird
That suddenly above the bees is heard,
The meteor that thrusts in with needle bill,
And off a blossom in mid air stands still.

For this is love and nothing else is love,
The which it is reserved for God above
To **sanctify** to what far ends He will,
But which it only needs that we fulfill.

ENGAGE

Why does the poem use "us" and "we" instead of "me" and "I"?

The "meteor" in stanza three clearly isn't a shooting star, so what might it be instead?

Does this prayer get answered?

IMAGINE

Regardless of the season, go outside and look at nature with a poet's eye for detail. What words and ideas come to mind?

DEFINE

dilating: *growing larger*

sanctify: *make holy*

THE OVEN BIRD

There is a singer everyone has heard,
Loud, a mid-summer and a mid-wood bird,
Who makes the solid tree trunks sound again.
He says that leaves are old and that for flowers
Mid-summer is to spring as one to ten.
He says the early petal-fall is past
When pear and cherry bloom went down in showers
On sunny days a moment overcast;
And comes that other fall we name the fall.
He says the highway dust is over all.
The bird would cease and be as other birds
But that he knows in singing not to sing.
The question that he frames in all but words
Is what to make of a **diminished** thing.

ENGAGE

Why does the poet personify the oven bird?

How is the work of the oven bird similar to the work of a poet?

Who or what is the "diminished thing"?

IMAGINE

Have you ever heard an oven bird? Listen to its unique song by searching "oven bird call" on YouTube or on Audubon.org.

Does its song change how you read or understand this poem?

DEFINE

Oven Bird: *small warbler bird*

diminished: *made smaller*

PART II

Innocence & Inspiration

IMAGINE

Poets make language memorable by creating unusual pairings of things. Pick two words at random from any book, then see how you might connect them in interesting ways.

 DEFINE

native: *original*

THE DOOR IN THE DARK

In going from room to room in the dark,
I reached out blindly to save my face,
But neglected, however lightly, to lace
My fingers and close my arms in an arc.
A slim door got in past my guard,
And hit me a blow in the head so hard
I had my **native** simile jarred.
So people and things don't pair any more
With what they used to pair with before.

HYLA BROOK

By June our brook's run out of song and speed.
Sought for much after that, it will be found
Either to have gone **groping** underground
(And taken with it all the **Hyla breed**
That shouted in the mist a month ago,
Like ghost of sleigh-bells in a ghost of snow)—
Or flourished and come up in jewel-weed,
Weak foliage that is blown upon and bent
Even against the way its waters went.
Its bed is left a faded paper sheet
Of dead leaves stuck together by the heat—
A brook to none but who remember long.
This as it will be seen is other far
Than with brooks taken otherwhere in song.
We love the things we love for what they are.

⚙ ENGAGE

What "song and speed" does a brook have?

Do words like "ghost" and "dead leaves" affect the mood of this poem?

What might this speaker want to write on the "faded paper sheet" of this brook?

💡 IMAGINE

Create a soundtrack for this poem. What songs fit the mood, style, and emotion?

🔤 DEFINE

groping: *searching blindly*

Hyla breed: *frog that sings during mating season*

29

ACQUAINTED WITH THE NIGHT

I have been one acquainted with the night.
I have walked out in rain—and back in rain.
I have outwalked the furthest city light.

I have looked down the saddest city lane.
I have passed by the **watchman** on his beat
And dropped my eyes, unwilling to explain.

I have stood still and stopped the sound of feet
When far away an interrupted cry
Came over houses from another street,

But not to call me back or say good-by;
And further still at an unearthly height,
One **luminary** clock against the sky

Proclaimed the time was neither wrong nor right.
I have been one acquainted with the night.

DESERT PLACES

Snow falling and night falling fast, oh, fast
In a field I looked into going past,
And the ground almost covered smooth in snow,
But a few weeds and stubble showing last.

The woods around it have it—it is theirs.
All animals are smothered in their lairs.
I am too absent-spirited to count;
The loneliness includes me unawares.

And lonely as it is that loneliness
Will be more lonely **ere** it will be less—
A blanker whiteness of **benighted** snow
With no expression, nothing to express.

They cannot scare me with their empty spaces
Between stars—on stars where no human race is.
I have it in me so much nearer home
To scare myself with my own desert place.

⚙ **ENGAGE**

Where does this poem seem to speed up? Slow down?

How does the poet make that happen?

What do you think are the speaker's own "desert places"?

💡 **IMAGINE**

Respond to this poem in art. Use paint, chalk, pencils, or crayons to express the emotions and illustrate the imagery.

📖 **DEFINE**

ere: *before*

benighted: *taken over by darkness*

BIRCHES

When I see birches bend to left and right
Across the lines of straighter darker trees,
I like to think some boy's been swinging them.
But swinging doesn't bend them down to stay
As ice-storms do. Often you must have seen them
Loaded with ice a sunny winter morning
After a rain. They click upon themselves
As the breeze rises, and turn many-colored
As the stir cracks and crazes their **enamel**.
Soon the sun's warmth makes them shed crystal shells
Shattering and avalanching on the snow-crust—
Such heaps of broken glass to sweep away
You'd think the inner dome of heaven had fallen.
They are dragged to the withered **bracken** by the load,
And they seem not to break; though once they are bowed
So low for long, they never right themselves:
You may see their trunks arching in the woods
Years afterwards, trailing their leaves on the ground
Like girls on hands and knees that throw their hair
Before them over their heads to dry in the sun.
But I was going to say when Truth broke in
With all her matter-of-fact about the ice-storm
I should prefer to have some boy bend them
As he went out and in to fetch the cows—
Some boy too far from town to learn baseball,
Whose only play was what he found himself,
Summer or winter, and could play alone.
One by one he **subdued** his father's trees

By riding them down over and over again
Until he took the stiffness out of them,
And not one but hung limp, not one was left
For him to conquer. He learned all there was
To learn about not launching out too soon
And so not carrying the tree away
Clear to the ground. He always kept his **poise**
To the top branches, climbing carefully
With the same pains you use to fill a cup
Up to the brim, and even above the brim.
Then he flung outward, feet first, with a swish,
Kicking his way down through the air to the ground.
So was I once myself a swinger of birches.
And so I dream of going back to be.
It's when I'm weary of considerations,
And life is too much like a pathless wood
Where your face burns and tickles with the cobwebs
Broken across it, and one eye is weeping
From a twig's having lashed across it open.
I'd like to get away from earth awhile
And then come back to it and begin over.
May no fate willfully misunderstand me
And half grant what I wish and snatch me away
Not to return. Earth's the right place for love:
I don't know where it's likely to go better.
I'd like to go by climbing a birch tree,
And climb black branches up a snow-white trunk
Toward heaven, till the tree could bear no more,
But dipped its top and set me down again.
That would be good both going and coming back.
One could do worse than be a swinger of birches.

ENGAGE

Who seems lonelier—the poem's speaker or the boy?

While this poem doesn't have a formal rhyme scheme, do you notice any repetition of sound and/or rhyme here? If so, where do you encounter it?

Why do you think "Toward" is in italics?

IMAGINE

This is a poem about self-discovery. What has helped you discover who you are? Art? Sports? Acting? Music? Poetry?

DEFINE

enamel: *hard surface*

bracken: *tall fern*

subdued: *triumphed over*

poise: *balance*

NOTHING GOLD
CAN STAY

Nature's first green is gold,
Her hardest **hue** to hold.
Her early leaf's a flower;
But only so an hour.
Then leaf subsides to leaf.
So **Eden** sank to grief,
So dawn goes down to day.
Nothing gold can stay.

ENGAGE

How can "Nature's first green" be gold?

Beyond being a precious metal and a color, what else might "gold" represent in this poem?

Why does the speaker reference the biblical garden of Eden?

IMAGINE

Try to memorize this short poem. Feel the shape of the words in your lungs and your mouth as you practice reciting it.

DEFINE

hue: *color*

Eden: *unspoiled paradise*

FLOWER-GATHERING

I left you in the morning,
And in the morning glow,
You walked a way beside me
To make me sad to go.
Do you know me in the **gloaming**,
Gaunt and dusty gray with roaming?
Are you **dumb** because you know me not,
Or dumb because you know?

All for me? And not a question
For the faded flowers **gay**
That could take me from beside you
For the ages of a day?
They are yours, and be the measure
Of their worth for you to treasure,
The measure of the little while
That I've been long away.

⚙ ENGAGE

Do you like when poems ask you questions? Do you try to answer them?

Does the "you" know why the speaker goes on walks?

If the speaker is Robert Frost, what is he gathering on these walks beyond flowers?

💡 IMAGINE

Sometimes a poem is a mirror. When you "look" into this mirror, what do you see about yourself?

What would you like to see?

🔤 DEFINE

gloaming: *twilight*

Gaunt: *very thin*

dumb: *silent*

gay: *bright*

THE NEED OF BEING VERSED IN COUNTRY THINGS

The house had gone to bring again
To the midnight sky a sunset glow.
Now the chimney was all of the house that stood,
Like a **pistil** after the petals go.

The barn opposed across the way,
That would have joined the house in flame
Had it been the will of the wind, was left
To bear forsaken the place's name.

No more it opened with all one end
For teams that came by the stony road
To drum on the floor with scurrying hoofs
And brush the **mow** with the summer load.

The birds that came to it through the air
At broken windows flew out and in,
Their murmur more like the sigh we sigh
From too much dwelling on what has been.

Yet for them the lilac renewed its leaf,
And the aged elm, though touched with fire;
And the dry pump flung up an awkward arm;
And the fence post carried a strand of wire.

For them there was really nothing sad.
But though they rejoiced in the nest they kept,
One had to be versed in country things
Not to believe the **phoebes** wept.

ENGAGE

Do you believe the wind meant to save the barn from the fire?

How do you think nature feels about this burned-down house?

What might it mean to be "versed in country things"?

IMAGINE

If you had to assign each stanza a color, what would you choose? And why?

DEFINE

pistil: *female reproductive parts of a plant*

mow: *stack of hay*

phoebes: *insect-catching birds*

PART III

Choice & Change

STOPPING BY WOODS ON A SNOWY EVENING

Whose woods these are I think I know.
His house is in the village though;
He will not see me stopping here
To watch his woods fill up with snow.

My little horse must think it **queer**
To stop without a farmhouse near
Between the woods and frozen lake
The darkest evening of the year.

He gives his harness bells a shake
To ask if there is some mistake.
The only other sound's the sweep
Of easy wind and **downy** flake.

The woods are lovely, dark and deep,
But I have promises to keep,
And miles to go before I sleep,
And miles to go before I sleep.

What do you imagine the woods might represent?

Is "the darkest evening of the year" the winter solstice, or something else?

What might happen if one slept in these woods?

IMAGINE

Think about a time when you were really interested in something, but responsibilities took you away from it. How did that feel?

How was your experience like or unlike this poem?

DEFINE

queer: *strange*

downy: *soft and fluffy*

FIRE AND ICE

Some say the world will end in fire,
Some say in ice.
From what I've tasted of desire
I hold with those who favor fire.
But if it had to perish twice,
I think I know enough of hate
To say that for destruction ice
Is also great
And would **suffice**.

ENGAGE

What do you think fire and ice represents in this poem?

How is it possible for a world "to perish twice"?

What answer does this poem offer regarding the fire/ice debate?

IMAGINE

To understand the power of line breaks, write out "Fire and Ice" as a single paragraph. How does this new prose version compare to the poem version?

Does the ending still have the same impact?

DEFINE

suffice: *be enough*

THE ROAD NOT TAKEN

Two roads diverged in a yellow wood,
And sorry I could not travel both
And be one traveler, long I stood
And looked down one as far as I could
To where it bent in the undergrowth;

Then took the other, as just as fair,
And having perhaps the better claim,
Because it was grassy and wanted wear;
Though as for that the passing there
Had worn them really about the same,

And both that morning equally lay
In leaves no step had **trodden** black.
Oh, I kept the first for another day!
Yet knowing how way leads on to way,
I doubted if I should ever come back.

I shall be telling this with a sigh
Somewhere ages and ages **hence**:
Two roads diverged in a wood, and I—
I took the one less traveled by,
And that has made all the difference.

ENGAGE

Are both roads "really about the same"?

Does this poem argue for taking one path over another?

Why does the speaker imagine telling this story "with a sigh" in the future?

IMAGINE

If you made this poem into a PowerPoint presentation, what images and music/ sound effects would you include?

DEFINE

trodden: *walked*

hence: *in the future*

AN OLD MAN'S WINTER NIGHT

All out-of-doors looked darkly in at him
Through the thin frost, almost in separate stars,
That gathers on the pane in empty rooms.
What kept his eyes from giving back the gaze
Was the lamp tilted near them in his hand.
What kept him from remembering what it was
That brought him to that creaking room was age.
He stood with barrels round him—at a loss.
And having scared the cellar under him
In **clomping** here, he scared it once again
In clomping off;—and scared the outer night,
Which has its sounds, familiar, like the roar
Of trees and crack of branches, common things,
But nothing so like beating on a box.
A light he was to no one but himsel
Where now he sat, concerned with he knew what,
A quiet light, and then not even that.
He **consigned** to the moon, such as she was,
So late-arising, to the broken moon
As better than the sun in any case
For such a **charge**, his snow upon the roof,
His icicles along the wall to keep;
And slept. The log that shifted with a jolt
Once in the stove, disturbed him and he shifted,
And eased his heavy breathing, but still slept.
One aged man—one man—can't keep a house,
A farm, a countryside, or if he can,
It's thus he does it of a winter night.

ENGAGE

Does it matter that the old man is forgetful?

How effective are walls, doors, windows, and floors at keeping away darkness and fear?

How does this being a "winter night" make it different than just a regular night?

IMAGINE

Read this poem every day for a week. What new details or nuances do you notice as you re-encounter the poem each time?

DEFINE

clomping: *walk heavily*

consigned: *confided*

charge: *claim*

MENDING WALL

Something there is that doesn't love a wall,
That sends the frozen-ground-swell under it,
And spills the upper boulders in the sun;
And makes gaps even two can pass **abreast**.
The work of hunters is another thing:
I have come after them and made repair
Where they have left not one stone on a stone,
But they would have the rabbit out of hiding,
To please the yelping dogs. The gaps I mean,
No one has seen them made or heard them made,
But at spring mending-time we find them there.
I let my neighbor know beyond the hill;
And on a day we meet to walk the line

And set the wall between us once again.
We keep the wall between us as we go.
To each the boulders that have fallen to each.
And some are loaves and some so nearly balls
We have to use a spell to make them balance:
'Stay where you are until our backs are turned!'
We wear our fingers rough with handling them.
Oh, just another kind of outdoor game,
One on a side. It comes to little more:
There where it is we do not need the wall:
He is all pine and I am apple orchard.
My apple trees will never get across
And eat the cones under his pines, I tell him.
He only says, 'Good fences make good neighbors.'
Spring is the mischief in me, and I wonder
If I could put a notion in his head:

'*Why* do they make good neighbors? Isn't it
Where there are cows? But here there are no cows.
Before I built a wall I'd ask to know
What I was walling in or walling out,
And to whom I was like to give offense.
Something there is that doesn't love a wall,
That wants it down.' I could say 'Elves' to him,
But it's not elves exactly, and I'd rather
He said it for himself. I see him there
Bringing a stone grasped firmly by the top
In each hand, like an old-stone **savage** armed.
He moves in darkness as it seems to me,
Not of woods only and the shade of trees.
He will not go behind his father's saying,
And he likes having thought of it so well
He says again, 'Good fences make good neighbors.'

ENGAGE

If the speaker truly doesn't want a wall, why do you think they keep repairing it?

What might this poem ultimately say about fences, walls, and boundaries?

How might this poem be about creativity? Or even writing a poem?

IMAGINE

If this poem were an egg, what might hatch from it if it got enough warmth and attention?

DEFINE

abreast: *side by side*

savage: *uncivilized person*

DUST OF
SNOW

The way a crow
Shook down on me
The dust of snow
From a hemlock tree

Has given my heart
A change of mood
And saved some part
Of a day I had **rued**.

ENGAGE

Is the crow an ominous presence here?

Was the crow's shaking of the snowy tree branch purposeful?

Do you think the speaker's mood changes for the better after having snow dumped on them?

IMAGINE

Change two verbs in "Dust of Snow." How does that affect the poem's meaning?

DEFINE

rued: *regretted*

THE FREEDOM OF
THE MOON

I've tried the new moon tilted in the air
Above a hazy tree-and-farmhouse cluster
As you might try a jewel in your hair.
I've tried it fine with little breadth of **luster**,
Alone, or in one ornament combining
With one **first-water** star almost shining.

I put it shining anywhere I please.
By walking slowly on some evening later,
I've pulled it from a crate of crooked trees,
And brought it over glossy water, greater,
And dropped it in, and seen the image **wallow**,
The color run, all sorts of wonder follow.

ENGAGE

Where do you notice alliteration (words close together that begin with the same sounds)?

Does the speaker truly have power over the moon?

What might the speaker really think about the moon?

IMAGINE

Imagine the moon's response to this poem. What does it think about its image wallowing? Its color running?

What action could the moon take?

DEFINE

luster: *reflective glow*

first-water: *highest grade of gem*

wallow: *settle underneath water*

THE WOOD-PILE

Out walking in the frozen swamp one gray day,
I paused and said, 'I will turn back from here.
No, I will go on farther—and we shall see.'
The hard snow held me, save where now and then
One foot went through. The view was all in lines
Straight up and down of tall slim trees
Too much alike to mark or name a place by

So as to say for certain I was here
Or somewhere else: I was just far from home.
A small bird flew before me. He was careful
To put a tree between us when he **lighted**,
And say no word to tell me who he was
Who was so foolish as to think what *he* thought.
He thought that I was after him for a feather—
The white one in his tail; like one who takes
Everything said as personal to himself.
One flight out sideways would have **undeceived** him.
And then there was a pile of wood for which
I forgot him and let his little fear
Carry him off the way I might have gone,
Without so much as wishing him good-night.
He went behind it to make his last stand.
It was a **cord** of maple, cut and split
And piled—and measured, four by four by eight.
And not another like it could I see.
No runner tracks in this year's snow looped near it.
And it was older sure than this year's cutting,
Or even last year's or the year's before.
The wood was gray and the bark warping off it
And the pile somewhat sunken. **Clematis**
Had wound strings round and round it like a bundle.
What held it though on one side was a tree
Still growing, and on one a stake and prop,
These latter about to fall. I thought that only
Someone who lived in turning to fresh tasks
Could so forget his handiwork on which
He spent himself, the labor of his ax,
And leave it there far from a useful fireplace
To warm the frozen swamp as best it could
With the slow smokeless burning of decay.

ENGAGE

Why do you think the speaker chooses to keep going? Are they seeking something so far from home?

What do you think the wood pile means to the speaker?

What might this poem say about decay?

IMAGINE

In what ways is this poem a mini-vacation?

Where does it take you?

What do you find when you go there?

DEFINE

lighted: *landed*

undeceived: *corrected*

cord: *stack of wood*

Clematis: *buttercup, a climbing plant*

Ten Things to Know About Robert Frost

1   Robert Lee Frost (1874–1963) was one of the most popular and respected poets of the twentieth century, despite his writing being largely ignored until he was nearly forty.

2   He received four Pulitzer Prizes and a US Congressional Gold Medal (the highest civilian award given by the government) for his poetry.

3   He was class poet and co-valedictorian of his high school with his future wife, Elinor White.

4   He received honorary degrees from Harvard and more than forty other institutions, despite never having graduated from college.

5   He wrote a poem called "Dedication" for the 1961 inauguration of John F. Kennedy. The sun was too bright for him to read off the page, so he recited "The Gift Outright" from memory instead.

6   Many of his poems were set in rural New England, where he lived for much of his adult life.

7   Since he outlived his sister, his wife, and four of his six children, death became a theme in many of his poems.

8   His poems often blended a traditional meter (patterns of syllables and stresses in poetry lines) with plain-spoken, everyday language.

9   He loved metaphors. Not only did he use them a lot in his poems, but the poems themselves were often metaphors.

10 He famously said, "A complete poem is one where an emotion has found its thought and the thought has found words."

Commentary on the Poems

PART I: EXPLORING NATURE

"Gathering Leaves"

Gathering leaves is a tedious task, and while it doesn't seem as vital as harvesting crops, it's all part of natural life cycles.

> NOTICE HOW THE TWO OPEN-ENDED QUESTIONS MAKE THIS POEM FAR MORE THAN JUST A COMPLAINT ABOUT YARD WORK.

"A Late Walk"

The walk described here occurs late in the year, which explains the dying plants and cold, soberness of the natural world.

> NOTICE HOW THE INTRODUCTION OF A "YOU" IN THE FINAL LINE CHANGES THE MOOD OF THIS POEM.

"Leaves Compared with Flowers"

While this poem compares leaves to flowers, it's also a metaphor for people and how we see one's outer beauty before recognizing inner beauty or value.

> NOTICE HOW THE SIZE OF THE MENTIONED PLANTS OR THE TIME OF DAY CAN REFER TO THE AGING PROCESS.

"My November Guest"

The speaker is very comfortable with a guest and doesn't want her to leave, even though she complains that she alone appreciates autumn.

> NOTICE HOW THE SPEAKER SHARES APPRECIATION FOR THE BEAUTY OF DESOLATE THINGS BUT KEEPS QUIET ABOUT THAT FACT.

"The Onset"

During a winter night, the speaker is momentarily feeling despair, but then recalls that seasons change and nature will prevail (as it always does).

> NOTICE HOW THERE'S QUIET OPTIMISM, DESPITE REFERENCES TO DARKNESS AND DEATH.

"Mowing"

The speaker tries to imagine what a scythe would say as it cuts grass. Ultimately, the work itself is far more important than any flight of the imagination.

> NOTICE HOW THIS POEM REINFORCES THE BELIEF THAT EVERYDAY THINGS ARE WORTHY SUBJECTS FOR POETRY.

"Tree at My Window"

The speaker never shuts the bedroom curtains because it'd block the sight of a beloved, dependable tree. Both speaker and tree seem to watch out for each other.

> NOTICE HOW NATURE IS OBSERVED WITHOUT THE SPEAKER BEING OUTDOORS—A RARE THING FOR A ROBERT FROST POEM.

"A Prayer in Spring"

Worried by the "uncertain harvest" ahead, the speaker looks upon the beauty of springtime and asks God to grant peace and happiness to everyone.

> NOTICE HOW THE JOYS OF SPRING (OR NATURE IN GENERAL) ARE PRESENTED AS LOVE.

"The Oven Bird"
In the middle of the woods in the middle of summer, an oven bird's song announces the passing of the season, which suggests the larger idea of the relentless passage of time.

NOTICE HOW THE REPETITION OF "FALL" MIGHT CONNECT WITH THE CHRISTIAN IDEA OF THE FALL OF ADAM (ORIGINAL SIN).

PART II: INNOCENCE & INSPIRATION

"The Door in the Dark"
The speaker accidentally walks into a door in the dark, and the resulting blow has them thinking differently.

NOTICE HOW INTRODUCING THE IDEA OF CREATING SIMILES (A FIGURE OF SPEECH THAT COMPARES TWO THINGS USING "LIKE" OR "AS") MAKES THIS A POEM ABOUT POEMS OR WRITING POETRY.

"Hyla Brook"
This ordinary brook used to have speed (flowing water) and sound (splashing), but here in June, it's all dried up. The speaker appreciates it for what it is instead of what it was or should be.

NOTICE HOW THIS BROOK MIGHT REPRESENT INSPIRATION AND HOW IT GOES UNDERGROUND FROM TIME TO TIME, BUT A POET KNOWS JUST WHERE TO LOOK.

"Acquainted with the Night"
While wandering the city at night, the speaker feels isolated as they recall a sense of sorrow that they've felt many times before.

NOTICE HOW THIS POEM IS ENTIRELY ABOUT THE MANMADE WORLD VERSUS THE NATURAL ONE. EVEN THE MOON IS A "LUMINARY CLOCK AGAINST THE SKY."

"Desert Places"
A nighttime snowstorm and the empty landscapes force the speaker to examine their own sense of loneliness.

NOTICE HOW "BENIGHTED" PLAYS ON BOTH ITS OLDER DEFINITION OF "SOMETHING TAKEN OVER BY DARKNESS" AND A MORE MODERN ONE ABOUT "INTELLECTUAL IGNORANCE."

"Birches"
The speaker sees birch trees "bend to the left and right" and imagines how they got that way, thinking the cause might be children on swings. Reason prevails, though—an ice storm likely caused the deformation.

NOTICE HOW THE POEM IS LIKE SWINGING, WHERE IT TRIES TO LIFT UP THROUGH NOSTALGIA AND IMAGINATION BUT IS PULLED BACK DOWN BY THE GRAVITY OF REALITY.

"Nothing Gold Can Stay"
All things fade, and that's as true for people as it is for nature where "nothing gold can stay."

NOTICE HOW "HER EARLY LEAF'S A FLOWER" IS BOTH A TRUE STATEMENT AND A USEFUL METAPHOR.

"Flower-Gathering"

A wife tags along for an early morning walk but heads home while the speaker continues on and picks flowers for them both.

"The Need of Being Versed in Country Things"

A house has burned to the ground some time ago, yet nature continues, undisturbed by human troubles.

PART III: CHOICE & CHANGE

"Stopping By Woods on a Snowy Evening"

At night during a snowfall, a traveler pauses to appreciate the silence but resumes the journey again because of "promises to keep."

"Fire and Ice"

This poem explores which end-of-the-world option is preferable—fire or ice.

"The Road Not Taken"

Faced with two paths ahead, the speaker chooses one route and wishes to later return to choose the other later, though they admit that's unlikely. Later, they'll falsely claim to have taken the less-traveled path.

"An Old Man's Winter Night"

An old, forgetful man living a solitary life surprisingly finds comfort in wintry darkness.

"Mending Wall"

When the speaker and a neighbor work together to fix a broken wall between their properties, the speaker suggests the wall is no longer needed, but the neighbor repeats the old saying: "Good fences make good neighbors."

"Dust of Snow"

After having a lousy day, the speaker's mood is changed when a bird shakes snow off a tree onto them.

"The Freedom of the Moon"

The speaker looks at, thinks about, and even relocates the moon, which shows how humankind has a freedom all their own.

NOTICE HOW THE ENDING DOESN'T REVEAL "ALL SORTS OF WONDER" CREATED BY THE IMAGE OF THE MOON IN WATER, WHICH INVITES READERS TO IMAGINE IT FOR THEMSELVES.

"The Wood-Pile"

During a walk through a frozen swamp, the speaker comes upon a long-abandoned stack of wood and wonders who'd create such a careful stack but then choose to leave it there.

NOTICE THE ROLE OF NATURE (THE BIRD AND THE PLANTS) HERE.

To Learn More About Robert Frost

1   *Papa Is a Poet: A Story About Robert Frost* by Natalie S. Bober. Henry Holt and Co., 2013.

Bibliography

1   www.poetryfoundation.org/poets/robert-frost

2   www.robertfrost.org

3   *Robert Frost: Collected Poems, Prose, and Plays.* Edited by Richard Poirier and Mark Richardson. Library of America, 1995.